SAY YES TO YOUTH!
DETROIT PUBLIC LIBRARY

Materials for the "Say YES to Youth"
Project were funded by a grant
from the Carnegie Foundation
to the Detroit Public Library.

Science Fair Projects Investigating Earthworms

Titles in the *Science Fair Success* series

Science Fair Success

Science Fair Projects Investigating Earthworms

Lloyd H. Barrow

Enslow Publishers, Inc.

40 Industrial Road   PO Box 38
Box 398   Aldershot
Berkeley Heights, NJ 07922   Hants GU12 6BP
USA   UK

http://www.enslow.com

To my daughter Valerie, who at a young age was fascinated with finding earthworms in the garden, and to her two children, Robert and Elizabeth.

Acknowledgments

I wish to thank Christina Owen, Brandi Owen, Amy Miles, and Karen Crawford, for typing this manuscript.

Library of Congress Cataloging-in-Publication Data

Barrow, Lloyd H.
     Science fair projects investigating earthworms / Lloyd H. Barrow.
        p. cm. — (Science fair success)
     Includes bibliographical references and index.
     Summary: Presents experiments, suitable for science fairs, that explore the structure, function, movement, preferences, and reactions of earthworms.
     ISBN 0-7660-1291-3
     1. Earthworms—Experiments Juvenile literature. 2. Science projects Juvenile literature.
[1. Earthworms—Experiments. 2. Experiments. 3. Science projects.] I. Title. II. Series.
QL391.A6B35   2000
592'.64—dc21   99-36381
                                              CIP

To Our Readers:
All Internet addresses in this book were active and appropriate when we went to press. Any comments or suggestions can be sent by e-mail to Comments@enslow.com or to the address on the back cover.

Illustration Credits: C. Ruth Neudahl

Photo Credits: Enslow Publishers, Inc.

Cover Illustration: Enslow Publishers, Inc.

Contents

Introduction

Right under your feet when you walk in your yard are hundreds of living animals. As you walk throughout the grass, insects such as beetles, grasshoppers, butterflies, and crickets may jump or fly away from you. But there are also many other small animals that crawl on or in the soil.

People who study living things are called biologists. People who study animals are called zoologists. Zoologists learn about animals by making careful observations. They ask questions and experiment to find the answers. Some of the questions they ask are easy to answer. To find out if a butterfly prefers yellow or red flowers, for example, they would observe how many butterflies are attracted to yellow and red flowers when the flowers are placed side by side. But some of the questions are trickier, such as "How did life form?" As scientists find answers to their questions, they come up with new questions and experiments.

This book is a collection of experiments that you can do at school or home. Doing them will help you to ask questions, find answers, and become a better observer. No one will ever know everything about biology—but it is great fun to learn as much as you can about living things.

Zoologists divide animals into two broad categories: vertebrates and invertebrates. Vertebrates are all animals that have backbones, like humans. Invertebrates, animals without backbones, are generally smaller types of animals. Earthworms are invertebrates and are the focus of this book of experiments.

To study animals, you must make detailed observations about the animal and its environment. *Environment* refers to the conditions necessary for the animal to live. Factors of the environment include temperature, amount of light, types of food available, and amount of moisture.

Science Fair Projects and the Scientific Method

This book is a collection of questions and experiments. Some of these experiments will introduce you to the behavior of earthworms in various environmental conditions. Others will help you understand how biologists study life. Many of these earthworm investigations could become science fair projects.

At a science fair, students display projects that they have conducted with the guidance of their teachers and parents. Your project should focus upon your interest or a scientific question you want to investigate and answer. Sometimes, the hardest part of a science fair project is deciding on the problem to solve. The following five questions will help you in conducting a science fair project:

What do I want to find out?
How can I find it out?
What materials do I need?
What do I think will happen?
What did happen and why?

By answering the above, you develop your problem, devise a way to investigate the problem, select the appropriate equipment to answer the problem, hypothesize what you think will happen, then collect and analyze your data to reach a conclusion. These are common steps biologists use in their research. Biologists think through the first four questions before starting. They also read to find out as much as they can about the topic. Then they are able to plan an experiment that will attempt to answer their question. Sometimes, their results do not match their hypothesis (what they think will happen). This does not mean their results were wrong. Biologists, like other scientists, repeat their experiments several times to be certain their results are consistent. Consistent results point to valid conclusions. The results of each science experiment help biologists in asking future questions.

The series of questions about earthworms in this book are appropriate for finding out information about earthworms and how they interact with their environment. Each experiment has five parts. The **materials list** tells you what you need. The opening statement of the investigation explains how to proceed to do the experiment safely. The **observations** suggest some of the things to look for. The **discussion** explains what your observations may tell you about biology. The **further investigations** suggests more questions and gives you ideas for science fair projects and about finding out more about biology.

Building an Earthworm Habitat

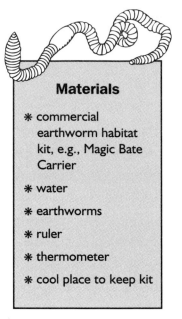

Materials

* ✳ commercial earthworm habitat kit, e.g., Magic Bate Carrier
* ✳ water
* ✳ earthworms
* ✳ ruler
* ✳ thermometer
* ✳ cool place to keep kit

Before starting your experiments with earthworms, you need to find some earthworms and make a proper habitat in which to care for them. The reason to build a habitat is so that you will not have to go outside to find an earthworm each time you want to do an experiment. Caring for a group of earthworms requires you to be responsible for their food and water supply and for their temperature. When you are finished with the earthworms, return them to their natural environment.

A commercial earthworm habitat kit will include bedding and food. The kit has ventilation areas so that there will be no odor. All you need to supply are the earthworms and water. The water you use in the habitat must first be left out in an uncovered container for twenty-four hours to allow any chlorine in it to evaporate.

To prepare the earthworms' habitat, similar to the one in Figure 1, fill the container with the water you prepared. After one minute, dump the water. Put bedding in the container up to 5 cm (2 in) from the top edge. Put the lid on the container and store in a place that is less than 10°C (50°F). Use a thermometer to check the temperature. For hot days, you can store the habitat in a refrigerator—after receiving a parent's permission.

Collect about twenty earthworms from your backyard or purchase them from a bait shop or pet store. Gently place the earthworms on top of the bedding. If the bedding sticks to the earthworms, add a small amount of water that has been left uncovered for twenty-four hours.

Spread two rows of earthworm food, which comes with the kit, along the length of the container. (In nature, earthworms eat decaying plants.) Each row should be 3 mm (1/8 in) wide. Each day check to see whether the food is eaten. When no food remains, replace with two rows again.

When you need earthworms for experiments, move the bedding around until you find them. When finished with the earthworms in the experiments, return them to the container unless directed otherwise.

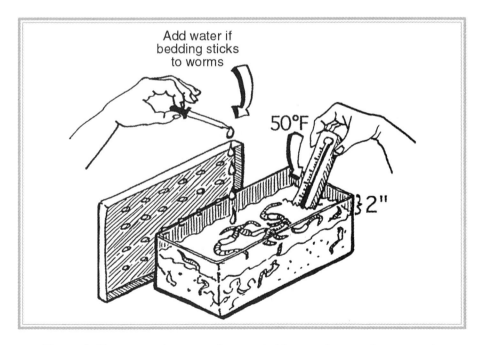

Figure 1. You can make an earthworm habitat so that you have a ready supply of earthworms for the experiments in this book.

Your habitat will be suitable for up to fifty earthworms. When you are finished raising your earthworms, dump the contents of the habitat in a place recommended by an adult (good examples would be a flower or garden area). Rinse the container with water and let it air dry before storing.

The worm bedding must be fluffy to allow for air exchange throughout the container, which helps prevent odor. Earthworms typically eat their own weight in food each day. They will also eat some of the bedding in the habitat. The amount of water in the habitat is very similar to the amount of water the earthworms store in their bodies. Your earthworms will reproduce, resulting in more earthworms than you put in at the start. In nature, earthworm numbers stay more consistent because some earthworms will die when eaten by enemies (e.g., birds and moles).

Safe Experimenting

1. Get an adult's permission before using anything in your home.
2. Ask an adult to watch you do the experiment. Grown-ups are interested in earth-living things, too!
3. Carefully follow the directions for each experiment.
4. Treat all living things with the same respect with which you would want to be treated.
5. Clean up when you are finished.
6. Treat the earthworms with care. Do not cause them any harm and return them to their habitat after you make your observations.
7. Have fun!

Chapter 1

Earthworm Structure and Function

Earthworms are commonly found in yards. Although most earthworms live in underground tunnels called burrows, they can also be found under piles of leaves or in your family's compost pile. They fit snugly in their burrows thanks to bristles, called setae, that run along the outside of their bodies. When they expand their bodies, they fit tightly in their burrow. If you try to remove them, they might break into two before they release their grip.

Since they are active mostly at night, earthworms are also known as night crawlers. They help break down the decaying matter in the soil, such as parts of dead plants and insects. As they move through the soil and ingest this material, they cast out soil rich in nutrients—castings—which plants can then use to grow. Besides providing rich material

as a fertilizer for plants, earthworms also loosen the dirt so that roots, water, and oxygen can spread through the soil.

Earthworms are long and thin, and they have no bones. Their bodies are constructed like two tubes, one inside the other. The inner tube digests its food and the outer tube is the worm's body wall. The smooth exterior of the body is made of rings, or segments, called annuli.

Earthworms also have no lungs. To breathe, they must take oxygen from the air around them through their damp skin into their blood vessels. Carbon dioxide moves out of the body in the same way. The blood travels through long blood vessels that run along the back and the underside of the earthworm. The earthworm has five pairs of muscular pumping tubes, called aortic arches, that act like hearts. They are near the head between the two long blood vessels.

In this chapter, you will be introduced to different parts of an earthworm's structures and functions, including the segments and setae, color, growth patterns, and benefits to soil.

Investigation 1

How many segments does an earthworm have?

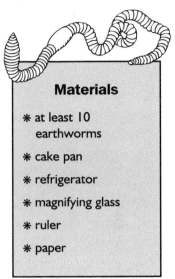

Materials

* at least 10 earthworms
* cake pan
* refrigerator
* magnifying glass
* ruler
* paper

Place an earthworm in the bottom of a cake pan, as shown in Figure 2. Notice a series of bumps called segments along the earthworm. If the earthworm is moving too much for you to make detailed observations, put it and its container in the refrigerator for two hours. This will not hurt the worm unless it is forgotten. Cooling the animal will slow its movement.

Measure the total length of the earthworm and, using a magnifying glass, count the number of segments. Record the length, color, and number of segments for at least ten earthworms. Note the differences between both ends of the earthworm. Gently touch an earthworm and describe how its skin feels.

Observations

What are the lengths of the longest and the shortest earthworm? How do the number of segments of the longest and shortest earthworms compare? Describe the colors and features of the earthworms.

When you are finished with the earthworms, put them in a location recommended by an adult, such as in the habitat or outside in their natural environment.

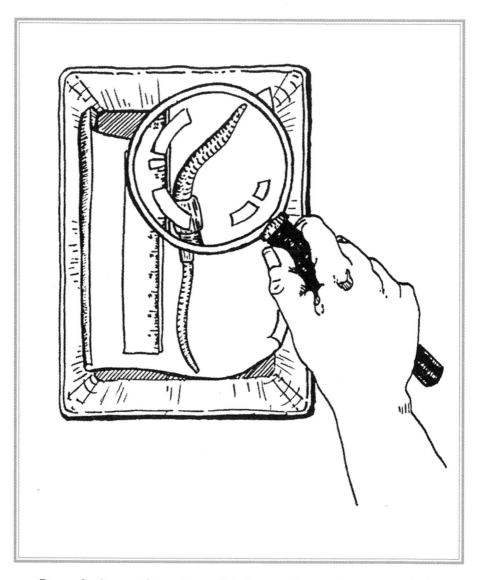

Figure 2. A magnifying glass will help you view each segment of the earthworm, especially young earthworms.

Discussion

Earthworms belong to the scientific group named annelids, which means "ringed." They are able to bend, squirm, reach up into the air, curl around things, and move forward and backward. As they move, it appears that they are first getting longer and thinner, then shorter and fatter, and back again. This flexible and streamlined movement pattern is due to the arrangement of the segments and helps earthworms move through the soil. They can tunnel around a buried rock rather than having to start a new burrow.

Each earthworm has both male and female reproductive systems. To form new earthworms, two earthworms must exchange sperm to fertilize each others eggs. After the earthworms exchange sperm, a mucous layer forms on the clitellum, the wide whitish band around the middle of the earthworm. This mucous layer case contains the fertilized eggs and is the length of a grain of rice. Muscle movements push the case off the anterior end of the earthworm. The case protects the fertilized eggs until they hatch, which generally takes several weeks. Colder temperatures result in a longer time to hatch. One of the ways that earthworms survive cold winters is by staying in the mucous layer case until the weather warms up.

Earthworms are long and thin with a soil-like color. Different colored earthworms are found in different colored soils. By being a similar color to their surroundings, earthworms have an advantage over their enemies. It is harder for their enemies to see them.

Further Investigations

What does it feel like when an earthworm crawls over your hand?

Measure the length of the clitella on at least ten earthworms to see whether long earthworms have long clitella.

Investigation 2

Why is it hard to pull an earthworm out of its burrow?

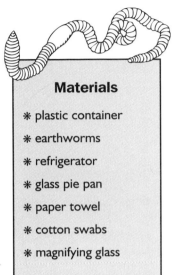

Materials

* plastic container
* earthworms
* refrigerator
* glass pie pan
* paper towel
* cotton swabs
* magnifying glass

Put a container of earthworms in the refrigerator for three hours so that they will be slower moving. Remove an earthworm and place it on its back in a pie pan lined with a damp paper towel so that you can see the underside of the earthworm. As shown in Figure 3, gently rub a cotton swab from the head to the tail on each side of the earthworm. Then rub the swab from the tail to the head on each side of a second earthworm.

Using the magnifying glass, look at several of the segments. Look for pieces of the cotton swab sticking to the earthworm.

Observations

What part of the earthworm has the most cotton sticking to it? Did more cotton stick to the earthworm that you rubbed from head to tail or the worm you rubbed from tail to head?

Discussion

Each segment of an earthworm, except the first and last, has four pairs of bristles (short stiff hairs) called setae. The setae help earthworms dig into the soil and cling to the sides of the burrow. When an earthworm puffs out, it fits tightly into its

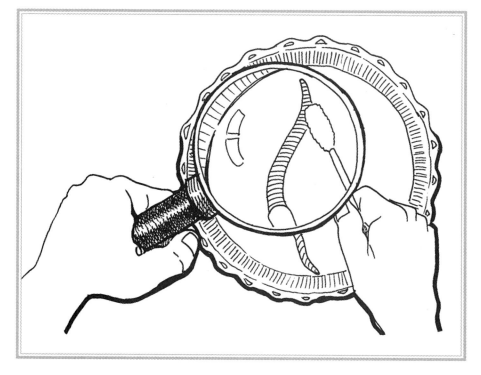

Figure 3. Rub a cotton swab on the underside of an earthworm. Use a magnifying glass to determine where the cotton sticks to the worm.

burrow, making it difficult for birds to pull them out. This grip is so strong that the earthworm will break before losing its hold. The presence of setae is why it is so difficult for a robin, even though it is much larger than the earthworm, to pull the worm out of the burrow.

Further Investigation

Repeat the cotton swab procedure when the earthworm is right side up. What differences do you notice?

Investigation 3

What part of an earthworm is most sensitive to light?

Materials

* flashlight
* sheet of cardboard
* pen
* scissors
* paper punch
* masking tape
* damp paper towel
* soda flat
* earthworms
* watch with second hand

Lay the head of a flashlight on a sheet of cardboard. Trace around the edge of the flashlight with a pen. Using scissors, cut around the drawn circle. Using a paper punch, punch a hole in the center of the cardboard circle. An adult can help you punch the hole if it is difficult to punch through the thick cardboard. Attach the cardboard to the head of the flashlight with masking tape. More than one thickness of masking tape may be needed to prevent light from shining around the edges of the cardboard.

Place a damp paper towel in a soda flat. Put an earthworm in the center of the box, as shown in Figure 4. Darken the room and wait for three minutes. Turn on the flashlight and shine it on the earthworm's tail and record what happens. You can tell the head from the tail of an earthworm. The segment at the tail is slightly flattened, and the segment at the head is not flattened. Turn off the flashlight for 30 seconds. Turn on the flashlight and shine it on the middle of the earthworm and record what happens. Turn off the flashlight and wait another 30 seconds. Now turn on the flashlight and shine the light on the earthworm's head and record what happens.

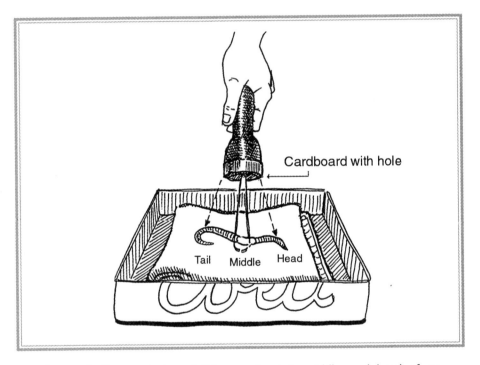

Figure 4. Shine a point of light on the tail, middle, and head of an earthworm. How does the earthworm react?

Observations

How did the earthworm react when light shone on its tail? Middle? Head?

Discussion

The small hole allows light to be concentrated in a small area and therefore allows you to see whether all parts of an earthworm's body react to light in the same way.

Earthworms usually come out of the ground at night. When you shine the flashlight on the earthworm's head, it wriggles away from the light. This occurs because there is a group of light-sensitive cells only near the head. After a few seconds, earthworms get used to the light. As shadows move across the ground and expose an earthworm to sunlight, the earthworm will burrow into the soil. If it did not move away from bright lights, it could dry up and die.

Further Investigation

Repeat the experiment, using bright and dim lights.

Investigation 4

How does an earthworm's color help it survive?

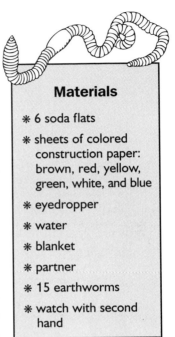

Cover the bottom of each of six soda flats with a different color construction paper. Put five drops of water in the center of each box. Put the boxes side by side so that they can be covered by a blanket, as shown in Figure 5.

Leave the room, then have a partner put 15 earthworms in the various boxes. Each box is to have at least one earthworm. Ask your partner to cover the boxes with a blanket. When you return to the room, your partner will uncover the boxes for ten seconds. Stand about a meter (3 feet) away from the boxes and count the earthworms you see in each box. After ten seconds, your partner should re-cover the boxes. Tell your partner how many earthworms you saw in each colored box. After sharing your observations, uncover the boxes and count the number of earthworms on each color of construction paper.

Observations

How many earthworms did you think were in the box lined with construction paper that was brown? Red? Yellow? Green? White? Blue? How many were actually there?

Which colors make it easiest to see the earthworms?

Figure 5. Here is a possible arrangement of earthworms in different colored backgrounds.

Discussion

One of the ways that earthworms avoid their enemies when on top of the ground is by matching the color of the soil. In different parts of the world, soil has different colors due to the different mineral contents. For example, reddish soil contains a very small amount of iron. In areas with this soil, earthworms tend to be reddish, because they are more difficult for their enemies to see.

Birds are one of the most common enemies of earthworms. Birds have very keen eyesight, especially when they see something move. Because earthworms are very slow moving, it is harder for birds to see them when they are a similar color to the background. As birds fly by, they will not notice the earthworms moving.

Further Investigations

Repeat the experiment, but uncover the boxes for 30 seconds.

Photograph each of the different-colored construction paper bottoms with earthworms. Show the photographs to a friend and see how many earthworms are observed in two seconds for each photo.

Investigation 5

What sounds does a moving earthworm make?

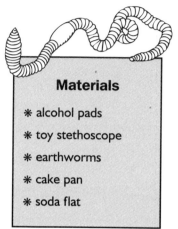

Materials

* alcohol pads
* toy stethoscope
* earthworms
* cake pan
* soda flat

Use an alcohol pad to sterilize the ear pieces of a toy stethoscope. Place the ear pieces in your ears and gently tap the end. If you do not hear the tapping, use another toy stethoscope.

Place an earthworm in a cake pan. Cover half the cake pan with a soda flat to provide a dark area. Put the stethoscope ear pieces in your ears and place the end piece against the bottom of the cake pan near the earthworm, as shown in Figure 6. Listen while the earthworm moves.

Observations

Describe the sounds the earthworm makes as it moves. What is the pattern to the sounds?

Discussion

The stethoscope was invented to provide a way of hearing sounds better. It focuses the sound directly into the wearer's ears.

The scraping sounds you heard are due to the bristles (short stiff hairs), called setae, found on the underside of the earthworm. Each segment of an earthworm except the first and last have four pairs of setae. Setae help earthworms dig

Figure 6. Listen to the sound that an earthworm makes when it crawls along the surface of the cake pan.

into the soil. The setae move at their own rate, independently of one another. If they moved at the same time, you would hear a pattern like scratch, space, scratch, space, scratch, space, and so on.

Further Investigation

Repeat the experiment, using a thin layer of soil for the earthworm to crawl on.

Investigation 6

How fast do earthworms grow?

Materials

* 5 empty coffee cans with lids
* potting soil
* ruler
* eyedropper
* water
* masking tape
* pen
* ice pick
* 5 earthworms
* food scale
* notebook
* newspaper
* an adult

Fill five coffee cans to within 2.5 cm (1 in) of the top with potting soil. Gently pat down the soil. Add ten drops of water to the top of the soil of each container. Using masking tape and a pen, make labels A, B, C, D, and E. Put a different label on each coffee can, as shown in Figure 7. **Have an adult** use an ice pick to punch three holes in each lid to let air into the can.

Pick an earthworm to go into container A. Before you put the earthworm in the container, record the length, the number of segments, and, using a food scale, the weight of the earthworm. Repeat the measuring, counting, and weighing of four more earthworms and place them in containers B, C, D, and E. Put the lid on each coffee can. Every three days, remove the lids, add five drops of water, and replace the lids.

Two weeks later, dump the soil in container A on a newspaper. Locate the earthworm and then measure it, count the number of segments, and weigh it. Repeat this for containers B, C, D, and E. Dump the soil and earthworms in a location recommended by an adult.

Figure 7. Fill five coffee cans with soil, water, and worms. After two weeks, how did the earthworms grow?

Observations

How much did the shortest earthworm grow over the two weeks?

How did the number of segments compare after two weeks?

How much weight did the earthworms gain over two weeks?

Discussion

Earthworms grow by having each segment get larger rather than adding segments. So the number of segments of your earthworm will be the same. Some small earthworms might appear to have grown more segments, but their segments are now more easily seen because they are larger.

The food scale may have recorded the weight of the earthworms in grams. As a reference, 1,000 grams, or one kilogram, is equal to 2.2 pounds. Some earthworms grow at a faster rate than others. They might be better burrowers and therefore take in more soil nutrients.

Further Investigations

Repeat the experiment, using a poor-quality soil (half potting soil and half sand, for example).

Repeat the experiment, using different kinds of earthworms (bloodworms, for example).

Investigation 7

How do earthworms affect water movement through the soil?

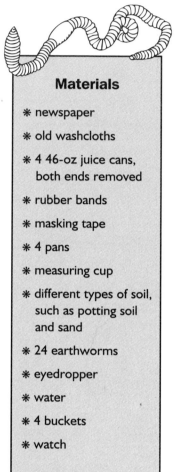

Materials

* newspaper
* old washcloths
* 4 46-oz juice cans, both ends removed
* rubber bands
* masking tape
* 4 pans
* measuring cup
* different types of soil, such as potting soil and sand
* 24 earthworms
* eyedropper
* water
* 4 buckets
* watch

If you are not outside, cover your experiment area with newspaper. Place pieces of old washcloth over one end of each of four juice cans that have had both ends removed. Hold the pieces in place with rubber bands. Then, using masking tape, tape the edges of the cloth around the cans. Put each juice can, covered end down, into separate pans (see Figure 8). Slowly add 500 ml (2 cups) of sand to two of the juice cans and 500 ml (2 cups) of potting soil to the other two juice cans. Gently shake the cans so that the soil is at the same height. Put 12 earthworms in one of the cans with soil and 12 in one of the cans with sand. Keep the other two cans free of worms. Label the cans. Cover the top of the cans with a newspaper. Leave them for eight days. Every other day add five drops of water to each can. After eight days, place the first can in a bucket. Slowly pour 250 ml (1 cup) of water into the juice can. After five minutes, carefully remove the can from the bucket and immediately dump the can's contents in a place

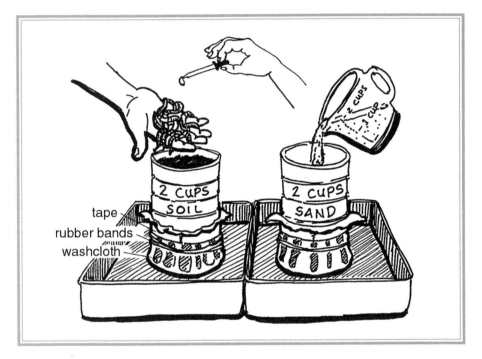

Figure 8. How do soil and sand differ in holding water? Eight days after you start this experiment, add 250 ml (1 cup) of water to find out.

recommended by an adult so that the earthworms will not drown. Pour the water from the bucket into a measuring cup. Measure and record how much water passed through this can. Repeat for the remaining three cans. Pour the water onto the ground, because the mixture could plug the sink.

Observations

How much water passed through each can?

Which can had the most water pass through it in five minutes?

Discussion

The space between the soil particles contains air that is used by earthworms and other living animals in the soil. When it rains, water goes into these spaces. Do the containers with burrowing earthworms hold more or less water than the containers without earthworms?

Water moves through different soils at different speeds. Scientists have found that the larger the soil particles, the faster the water passes through. Sand particles are large and uneven, so they do not fit close together, and water passes through easily. Soil particles, on the other hand, have small particles that slow water movement through them. Scientists will frequently describe a soil as porous (having lots of space) or not porous. They are referring to the soil's porosity, or the amount of air space between the soil particles.

As you can see, the composition of a soil affects how fast water soaks into it. Permeability is the rate at which water goes through the soil. Scientists describe soils through which water passes quickly as being permeable. Usually, the more firmly packed the soil, the slower water passes through. Water goes through sandy soils faster than through silt or clay soils.

Further Investigations

Repeat the experiment, using 500 ml (2 cups) of water.

Repeat the experiment, using 25 earthworms in each can.

Investigation 8

How does a bird's color vision help earthworms survive?

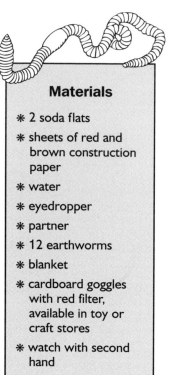

Materials

* * 2 soda flats
* * sheets of red and brown construction paper
* * water
* * eyedropper
* * partner
* * 12 earthworms
* * blanket
* * cardboard goggles with red filter, available in toy or craft stores
* * watch with second hand

Cover the bottom of one soda flat with red construction paper and the bottom of another with brown construction paper. Put five drops of water in the center of each box. Put the boxes side by side so that they can be covered by a blanket.

Leave the room and have a partner divide 12 earthworms between the two boxes. Each box should have at least four earthworms. Your partner should cover the boxes with a blanket. Before going into the room, put on goggles with red filters. After entering the room, have your partner uncover the boxes for ten seconds (see Figure 9). Observe and record the number of earthworms you saw in each box. After recording the number, compare the number you saw with the actual number of earthworms in each box.

Leave the room and have your partner redivide the earthworms between the boxes. After the boxes are covered with the blanket, enter the room without the goggles. Have your partner uncover the boxes for ten seconds, and record what you see. Then compare the number of earthworms you saw with the actual number in each box.

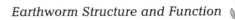

Figure 9. Wearing red-filter glasses makes it harder to see things on different colored backgrounds.

Observations

How did the filter affect the number of earthworms you were able to see on the red and brown construction paper?

On which color of construction paper was it easier to see the earthworms?

Discussion

Besides the ability to blend in with the environment, like the earthworm on brown paper, survival depends on being able to reproduce. Earthworms that match closely the color of the local soil will probably survive and mate with similar-colored earthworms, producing similar-colored earthworm offspring. Sometimes earthworms are brought from other areas, and they do not match the soil color well. More of these earthworms will be seen by enemies such as birds and be eaten. Survival means not just living, but living to reproduce.

We see an object when light strikes the object and is reflected to our eyes. White light from any source is composed of seven different colors. Red is one of the colors of the spectrum. The purpose of the filter in this experiment is to block out that color from reaching our eyes. What is reflected is all colors except red, like a bird would see.

Birds have a field of vision that requires them to look from side to side to be able to see a wide area. Their keen eyesight will pick out moving objects better than nonmoving things. Consequently, the slow movement rate of earthworms is frequently missed. This gives earthworms a greater likelihood of surviving and reproducing.

Further Investigations

Repeat the experiment, using sunglasses.

Repeat the experiment, using a different colored filter.

Chapter 2

Earthworm Movement

An earthworm's body wall has two layers of muscles under its skin. One layer runs the length of the body, from head to tail. These longitudinal muscles can shorten or lengthen the worm. The second set surrounds the width of the earthworm. When these circular muscles contract, the earthworm shrinks or spreads out. To inch its way through the soil, an earthworm uses both sets of muscles, one to push through the soil, and one to pull its hind end up. The setae on the outside of the earthworm prevent it from slipping.

This chapter presents some investigations that you can use to learn more about how an earthworm moves: How fast does an earthworm move? Does temperature affect how fast they move? How fast does an earthworm burrow in different types of soil?

Investigation 9

How fast does an earthworm move?

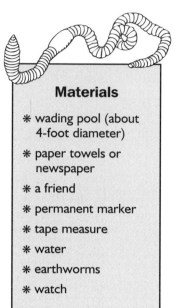

Materials

* wading pool (about 4-foot diameter)
* paper towels or newspaper
* a friend
* permanent marker
* tape measure
* water
* earthworms
* watch

Place a wading pool on a level surface. Lay paper towels or newspaper over the entire bottom of the pool. With a friend's help, use a permanent marker to draw a series of consecutive circles with a diameter of 25 cm (10 in), 50 cm (20 in), 75 cm (30 in), and 100 cm (40 in) from the center of the pool on the paper towels or newspaper (see Figure 10). Dampen the paper towels or newspaper with water. Place earthworms at the center of the wading pool and time how long it takes them to reach each circle.

Observations

How long did it take for an earthworm to reach the 25-cm (10-in) mark? 50-cm (20-in) mark? 75-cm (30-in) mark? 100-cm (40-in) mark? Calculate their speed in centimeters (or inches) per minute. Can you convert their speed to miles per hour?

Discussion

The distance earthworms move in one series of getting longer and shorter is very short. An earthworm is moving fast when it goes 17 cm (12 in) in two minutes. Earthworms do not

Figure 10. Draw concentric circles on paper before putting earthworms at the center of the wading pool.

travel in straight lines, either. So your earthworms might take a long time to reach the 100-cm (40-in) circle. It has been estimated that it would take about three days for an earthworm to travel half a mile.

Further Investigations

Raise one end of the pool with a long board. How does this affect the direction earthworms move? Do they tend to move downhill or uphill?

Investigation 10

How does temperature affect how fast earthworms move?

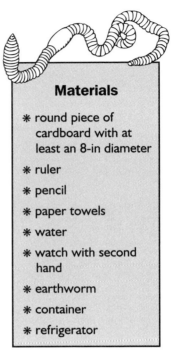

Materials

* round piece of cardboard with at least an 8-in diameter
* ruler
* pencil
* paper towels
* water
* watch with second hand
* earthworm
* container
* refrigerator

Using your ruler and pencil, draw a line from one edge to the opposite edge of a round piece of cardboard through the center. Turn the cardboard one quarter of a turn and draw another line. The place where the lines cross is the center of the cardboard. Mark a bold **X** at this center, as shown in Figure 11. Cover the entire cardboard circle with wet paper towels. If the X cannot be seen through the wet towels, make it darker.

Lay an earthworm over the X and time how long in seconds it takes the earthworm to reach the edge of the cardboard circle. Repeat for a total of five trials, then average the time. To find the average, add the total number of seconds, then divide by the number of trials.

Place the earthworm in a container and put it in the refrigerator for two hours. Remove the earthworm and do five more trials.

Observations

Before it was put in the refrigerator, what were the fastest and slowest times for the earthworm to reach the edge of the

Figure 11. Locate the center of a cardboard disk and mark it with an X. Place an earthworm at the center of the cardboard.

cardboard? After being in the refrigerator, what were the fastest and slowest times for the earthworm to reach the edge? How do the two averages compare?

Discussion

Earthworm activity is influenced by the temperature of the earthworm's environment. Usually, earthworms move slower on cooler days. Also, they move slower during the coolest parts of a day. When an earthworm gets too hot, the moist body layer will dry up and the worm will die.

The reason for taking five trials under each condition is that sometimes an earthworm will not go in a straight line to the edge. Also, earthworms travel at a slow rate. The multiple trials and the average provide a better estimate of how long it will typically take an earthworm to reach the edge. The more trials you do, the more accurate your results will be. This is why a scientist repeats each experiment many times.

Further Investigations

Repeat the experiment after the earthworm has been in the refrigerator for 30 minutes, 1 hour, and 4 hours. Do not keep it in any longer than 4 hours. How do the results vary?

Place some ice cubes in a cup next to an earthworm and observe what happens.

Investigation 11

How fast does an earthworm burrow in different types of soil?

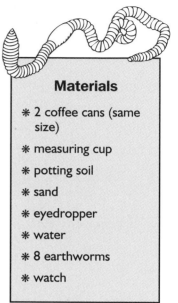

Materials

* 2 coffee cans (same size)
* measuring cup
* potting soil
* sand
* eyedropper
* water
* 8 earthworms
* watch

Use only clean, dry cans for this experiment. Put 4 cups of potting soil in a coffee can. Place 4 cups of sand in a second coffee can. Gently press down on the contents in each can until firm, as shown in Figure 12. Add five drops of water to each can. Place an earthworm on the top surface of each can. Make sure both earthworms are of equal length. Record the time it takes until each earthworm begins to burrow. Then record how long it takes until it is fully covered with soil. Repeat the procedure separately with three other pairs of equally sized earthworms. When you are done, dump the contents of the cans in a place recommended by an adult, such as your flower garden.

Observations

What was the shortest time for an earthworm to start to burrow? What was the longest time it took for an earthworm to be completely covered with soil? With sand?

Discussion

Earthworms burrow at different rates. Usually it takes longer to burrow into clay because the individual grains of clay fit

(a)   (b)

} fill with soil
to within 2 cm
of top

} fill with sand
to within 2 cm
of top

Figure 12. a) Add soil or sand to empty coffee cans and gently tap them down. b) Add five drops of water to each can. Then add a worm to each can. The worms should be of equal size.

closer together and make it harder for the earthworm to dig. It is easier for earthworms to make their burrows in moist soil. An earthworm digs by pushing aside the soft soil particles and expanding its body to push them farther aside. Then, the earthworm pulls its body into the burrow, which can be either long and straight or U shaped. The linings of burrows are made of soft soil and smooth stones. Frequently, earthworms will plug the opening to their burrow with leaves. This plug reduces the chance of enemies and rain entering the burrow.

When earthworms are making their burrows, they are also helping others. Burrowing in the soil makes tunnels that allow air and water to enter when it rains. The air and water supply underground animals and plants with these materials. While burrowing, an earthworm mixes the soil, breaks it up, and adds nutrients to it. The body wastes of earthworms provide a natural fertilizer to the soil. Frequently, growing plant roots follow the paths of earthworm burrows.

Further Investigations

Compare the burrowing speed through two other types of packed soil.

How does the burrowing speed compare when the soil mixture is half potting soil and half sand? Half vermiculite? Half peat moss?

Investigation 12

How fast does an earthworm burrow in topsoil and subsoil?

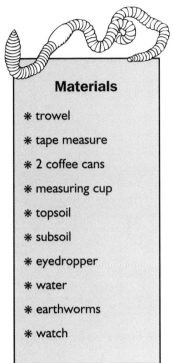

Materials

* trowel

* tape measure

* 2 coffee cans

* measuring cup

* topsoil

* subsoil

* eyedropper

* water

* earthworms

* watch

Using a trowel, dig a hole straight down in the ground, at least 38 cm (15 in) deep. Be sure to ask an adult to let you know where you may dig. Looking into the hole, notice the different colored layers in the soil. If there is no color change, dig deeper. The dark layer near the surface is called topsoil. The lighter layer that is below the topsoil is called subsoil. If there are no layers, the soil has been mixed, which happens when houses are built. If this is the case, you will need to dig in another location.

Use only clean, dry coffee cans of the same size for this experiment. Put 4 cups of topsoil in one can. Place 4 cups of subsoil in the other can. Gently press down on the soil in each can until firm. Add five drops of water to each can. Place an earthworm on the top surface of each can, as shown in Figure 13. Make sure the earthworms are of equal length. Record the time it takes until each earthworm begins to burrow and then until it is fully covered with soil. Compare how the earthworms burrow in each can of soil. When you are done, dump the contents of the cans in the hole that you dug.

Figure 13. Locate topsoil and subsoil and put 4 cups of each in separate coffee cans. How does the soil type affect the burrowing rate of an earthworm?

Observations

In which type of soil do the earthworms burrow the fastest? In which type of soil do they burrow the slowest?

Discussion

Topsoil usually contains large numbers of earthworms, whereas the subsoil usually has no or very few earthworms. Topsoil is less compacted and is easier for the earthworms to burrow in. The dark color of the topsoil indicates organic matter (dead plants), which is a source of food for earthworms. Subsoil lacks organic matter.

Due to the compaction of the subsoil, earthworms must eat their way through by opening their mouths and collecting soil. They swallow the soil and it is digested and passed out as waste in small pellets, called castings. Burrowing in the subsoil helps the very slow process of changing subsoil into topsoil.

Further Investigations

Repeat the experiment with the subsoil and topsoil mixed together in a third container.

Repeat the experiment when more water (16 drops, for example) is used.

Investigation 13

How fast can an earthworm finish a T-maze?

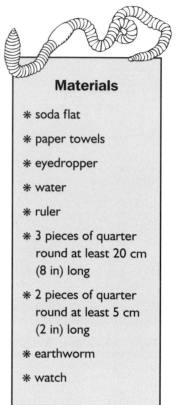

Materials

* soda flat
* paper towels
* eyedropper
* water
* ruler
* 3 pieces of quarter round at least 20 cm (8 in) long
* 2 pieces of quarter round at least 5 cm (2 in) long
* earthworm
* watch

Cover the bottom of a soda flat with two layers of paper towels. Add three drops of water to the center of the box. Arrange three pieces of 20-cm (8-in) quarter round and two pieces of 5-cm (2-in) quarter round, as shown in Figure 14. If you are not able to obtain these pieces in these exact lengths, **ask an adult** to help you cut the quarter rounds to the correct lengths. When you look down on the box, the inside of the quarter round pieces should look like a T.

Put the earthworm at the bottom end of the T, with its head facing the top of the T. Record whether it turns left or right when it gets to the top of the T. Record how long it takes it to travel through the maze. When it reaches the end, put it at the bottom again and time how long it takes to travel the maze.

Observations

How long did it take for the earthworm to travel the maze?

Did the earthworm turn to the left or to the right?

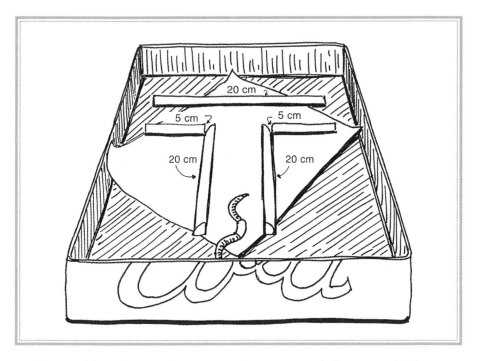

Figure 14. A T-maze for your earthworms can help you study their movement patterns.

How does the second time compare with the first time?

Discussion

Earthworms do not always turn the same direction in a maze. Sometimes a food odor will attract them in a particular direction. Zoologists are unsure whether earthworms can be trained to turn only to the left or to the right. Earthworms tend to follow their previous trail.

Further Investigations

Under adult supervision, put one drop of diluted ammonia at either the left or right opening of the T to see how an earthworm reacts.

Repeat the experiment, using five other earthworms to see whether or not they follow the first earthworm's path or not.

Chapter 3

Earthworm Environments

Earthworms, like all animals, tend to live in environments that have the best living conditions. Besides avoiding their enemies, earthworms need a source of food, proper temperature, and proper amount of moisture. These environmental factors will determine whether earthworms will flourish or not.

You may already know that an earthworm is a preferred dietary staple for birds, moles, and frogs. But do you know what earthworms prefer to eat? Do you know whether they like wet or dry soil? Continue with the experiments in this chapter to find the answers to these and other questions.

Do earthworms prefer a wet or dry environment?

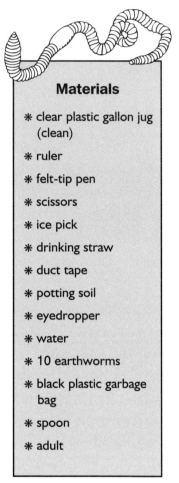

Materials

* clear plastic gallon jug (clean)
* ruler
* felt-tip pen
* scissors
* ice pick
* drinking straw
* duct tape
* potting soil
* eyedropper
* water
* 10 earthworms
* black plastic garbage bag
* spoon
* adult

Measure 20 cm (8 in) up from the bottom of a clear plastic gallon jug on all sides. Mark this height with a felt-tip pen. Draw a line around the jug that connects the dots. **With an adult's assistance,** cut along the line, as shown in Figure 15. Discard the top of the jug. Turn the jug on its side. Measure 5 cm (2 in) up from the bottom and make a dot with the pen on one side. **Have an adult** use an ice pick to punch a hole at the dot large enough to insert a drinking straw. Put the straw through the hole so that 2.5 cm (1 in) of the straw is inside the jug. Measure 2.5 cm (1 in) on the straw from the outside of the jug and cut off the excess. Seal around the straw with duct tape to hold the straw in place, as shown in Figure 16a.

Carefully add potting soil until the soil is 2.5 cm (1 in) from the top of the jug. Add ten drops of water to the top of the soil and eight drops through the straw. You will need to squeeze the eyedropper hard to force the water through the straw and inside the jug. Put ten earthworms on the top of the soil and put the jug in a black plastic garbage bag, as

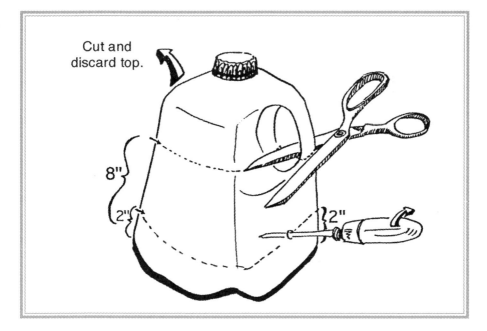

Figure 15. An empty jug will become an experimental home for your earthworms. You can then find out if they like a wet or a dry environment.

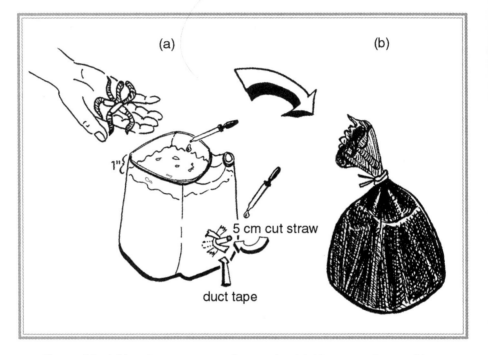

Figure 16. a) Use duct tape to seal around a drinking straw inserted into the jug. Add ten drops of water to the top of the soil in the jug and eight drops through the straw. Then add ten earthworms. b) Place the jug into a black garbage bag and check it after three, six, nine, and twelve days.

shown in Figure 16b. Put the container in a cool area for three days.

After three days, remove the jug from the bag and look for earthworms and their burrows on all sides of the jug. Record your observations. Add five drops of water through the straw. Replace the jug in the plastic bag. Repeat the checking and adding of water on days six, nine, and twelve. Thirteen days after starting this experiment, remove the jug. Carefully remove the soil from the jug with a spoon in the following way: Remove the top 5 cm (2 in) as a layer. Make observations about the number of earthworms and burrows in this top 5 cm (2 in). Now remove the soil vertically on the side opposite the straw. Record your observations about the number and location of earthworms and burrows. Remove the duct tape and straw. Then remove the soil from where the straw was located. Record the number of earthworms and location of burrows.

Observations

What did you see at day three? Day six? Day nine? Day twelve?

When you removed the soil from the jug, where was the greatest number of earthworms found?

Discussion

Earthworms prefer an environment that has large amounts of organic matter as a food source. Also, they prefer a damp area, not a dry or wet area. The damp area helps keep the moist body covering (mucus) of the earthworms' skin slimy. Placing the water in a certain area of the jug will usually attract earthworms to that damp area.

If you accidentally cut an earthworm into two, do not be greatly concerned, because earthworms have the ability to regenerate (grow back) cut parts. These new parts will work just as well as the original. Regeneration will occur faster in the first and last four segments.

Further Investigation

Repeat the experiment with two straws, the second one 5 cm (2 in) higher than the first.

Investigation 15

What type of soil do earthworms prefer?

Materials

* magnifying glass
* potting soil
* sandbox sand
* ruler
* 2 soda flats
* masking tape
* measuring cup
* eyedropper
* water
* 10 earthworms
* watch

The dark color of potting soil is due to the mixture of organic matter, including dead plants and topsoil. Use a magnifying glass to examine the soil particles in the potting soil.

Examine the size of sand particles. The size is important because sand, silt, and clay are classified according to their size. Sand particles are at least 2 millimeters in diameter. Silt and clay are smaller. Using the magnifying glass, examine the edges of the sand particles.

Lay a ruler on its edge across the width of a soda flat. Use masking tape to hold the ruler in place, as shown in Figure 17. Measure one cup of potting soil and dump it next to the left side of the ruler. Measure one cup of sand and dump it next to the right side of the ruler. Add five drops of water to each the potting soil and sand. Put ten earthworms on the ruler. Lay a second soda flat over the first flat.

Lift the second box after 1, 5, and 10 minutes to check to see how many earthworms are on the potting soil and how many are on the sand. Each time, cover the box again. After ten minutes, spread out the potting soil and count how many earthworms went to the potting soil side. Spread out

Figure 17. Place earthworms on a ruler between piles of sand and potting soil. Which do they like better?

the sand and count how many earthworms went to the sand side.

Observations

Which type of soil has the most earthworms on top of it after 1 minute? 5 minutes? 10 minutes?

Discussion

Potting soil tends to absorb water better and hold on to it longer than sand. By placing the same number of drops of water on each side, you are trying to conduct a controlled experiment. The reason for checking the earthworms' locations at various times is that all earthworms do not move at the same speed. Usually, after ten minutes, more earthworms will be found in the potting soil than in the sand. Potting soil has more organic matter and may have an odor that attracts earthworms.

Sand particles can have various shapes. New sand particles have sharp square corners, whereas sand found near a river, a lake, or an ocean will have been worn smooth by the moving water. The smaller the soil particles, the slower the water moves through a thick layer of the soil. Typically, water will move faster through layers of sand than through layers of clay or silt because there is more space between sand particles than between clay or silt particles. This air space allows for easier water movement.

Further Investigations

Repeat the experiment, using clay soil and potting soil.

Repeat the experiment, using clay soil and sand.

Investigation 16

What kind of food do earthworms like best?

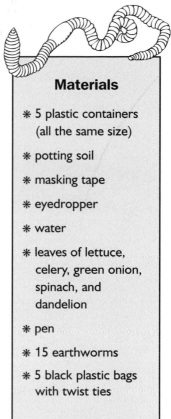

Materials

* 5 plastic containers (all the same size)
* potting soil
* masking tape
* eyedropper
* water
* leaves of lettuce, celery, green onion, spinach, and dandelion
* pen
* 15 earthworms
* 5 black plastic bags with twist ties

Fill five equally sized plastic containers two-thirds full with potting soil. Attach a piece of masking tape to each container. Add eight drops of water to each container. Place a lettuce leaf in one container, a celery leaf in the second, and green onion, spinach, and dandelion leaves separately in the third, fourth, and fifth containers. Try to make sure the size of all leaves is the same. Label each cup with the type of leaf it contains, as shown in Figure 18a. Place three earthworms in each container and put the containers separately inside black plastic bags. Use a twist tie to close each bag, as shown in Figure 18b. Place the bags in a cool, quiet area for two days.

After two days, remove the containers from the bags and compare how much of each leaf is left. After making observations, dump the containers in a location recommended by an adult.

Observations

What were the most common leaves eaten? The least common?

Figure 18. a) Add eight drops of water to each container. Then add three worms to each. b) Place each container into a black plastic garbage bag and keep them in a cool, quiet area for two days. What do you observe when they are uncovered?

Discussion

Using three worms in each container helped you verify that your observations were correct. Just like humans, some earthworms like one kind of leaf and others prefer different kinds of leaves.

Usually, earthworms prefer leaves that do not have a strong odor and have a high amount of moisture. The moist leaves are easier for the earthworms to chew and swallow.

Earthworms will also eat dried leaves. Their preference for tree leaves is different for fresh and dried leaves. For example, earthworms prefer fresh tree leaves in the following order: beech, maple, oak, and willow. The order of preference of dried leaves is willow, oak, beech, and maple.

Further Investigations

Repeat the experiment with leaves from various flowering plants.

Repeat the experiment, this time shredding the leaves and adding 20 equal-sized pieces to each container. Did the smaller size of the plants make a difference?

Chapter 4

Earthworm Reactions

Earthworms are less complex than humans. For example, they have no eyes. How do you think they know where they are going? How do they know when it is light out? Earthworms do not have ears. Do you think they need to "hear" things? Their brain consists of a cluster of nerve tissue near the front end of their bodies. Do you think they can remember where they have been?

In this chapter you will investigate the answers to many questions, including: Do earthworms prefer light or darkness? How do earthworms react to acid rain? How does excess water affect earthworms?

How do earthworms react to light and darkness?

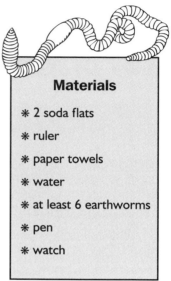

Materials

* 2 soda flats
* ruler
* paper towels
* water
* at least 6 earthworms
* pen
* watch

Measure the length of one soda flat and find the middle. Put a dot there. Draw a line across the width of the soda flat through the dot, as shown in Figure 19a. Place wet paper towels on the bottom of the soda flat. Turn over the second soda flat and cover exactly half of the bottom box by placing the cover directly over the line across the bottom box (see Figure 19b). Put several earthworms at the line and check to see where they are at 1, 3, 5, 10, and 15 minutes.

Observations

How many earthworms were in the dark after each time interval? How many were in the light after each interval?

Discussion

Earthworms usually spend most of their lives underground in burrows (tunnels made by earthworms). They tend to move away from light. Earthworms do not have eyes, but their bodies are sensitive to light and vibrations. They avoid light because light tends to dry out their skin and causes them to die. The reason for checking the earthworms' position at various times is that earthworms do not always move at the

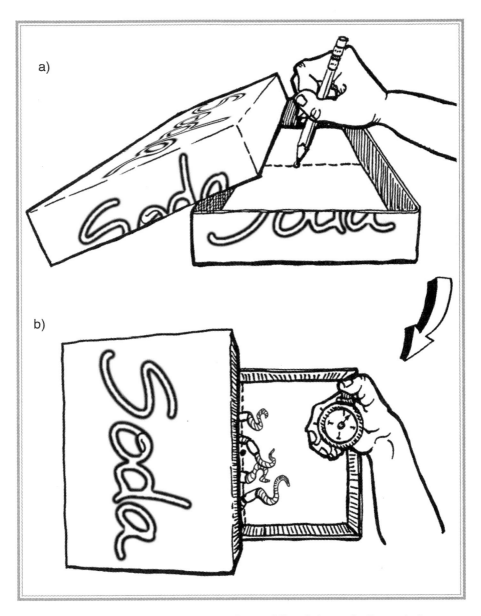

Figure 19. a) Draw a line across the middle of the soda flat and place another flat over half of the first one. b) Place the earthworms on the midline of the flat. Do they tend to go toward the light or the dark?

same speed. Sometimes an earthworm will stay in the area where it was originally placed. Sometimes it will come to the surface of the ground shortly after sunrise to feed or mate. Usually, within two hours after sunrise, earthworms have returned to their burrows.

Further Investigation

Repeat the experiment, using a flashlight in a dark area. How do earthworms react to the light?

Investigation 18

How do earthworms react to touch?

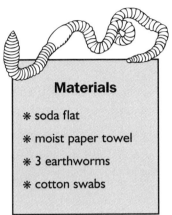

Materials

* soda flat
* moist paper towel
* 3 earthworms
* cotton swabs

Place a moist paper towel in a soda flat. Place a single earthworm in the center of the box, as shown in Figure 20. Using a cotton swab, gently touch the head of the earthworm and record how the earthworm reacts. (The head of an earthworm is thicker than the tail.) Repeat the procedure for the middle of the back and tip of the tail of the earthworm.

Put the earthworm back in the habitat, and repeat the experiment with two other earthworms.

Observations

How did the earthworm move after being touched? Which part of the earthworm reacted fastest when touched?

Discussion

Earthworms have a mouth and a very sensitive head that helps them find their food (decaying matter). The skin of an earthworm is very sensitive. It is used to see, hear, detect moisture, and feel textures and vibrations. Usually, the entire skin is equally sensitive to touch.

The earthworm is not able to move away from your touch with one movement. This is because an earthworm has only two sets of muscles. One set is the circular muscles located

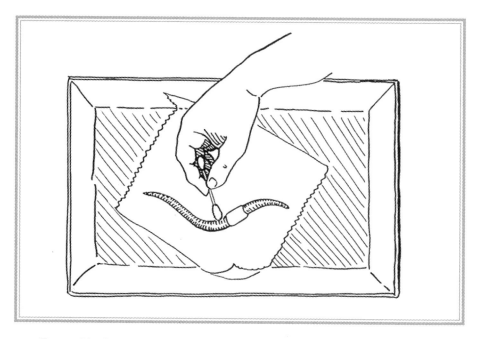

Figure 20. Gently touch a cotton swab to the head, middle, and tail of an earthworm. How does the earthworm react?

around each of the segments of the earthworm. The other set is the long muscles that go from the head to the tail. These muscles give earthworms an unusual movement pattern. When the circular muscle tightens, the earthworm becomes longer and thinner. When the long muscles tighten, it becomes shorter and fatter. This squeezing together followed by stretching out is how an earthworm moves from one place to another. An earthworm can also move backward. Regardless of where you touch the earthworm, both sets of muscles will cause it to move away.

Further Investigations

What happens when the head of an earthworm encounters a hard object?

What happens when the tail encounters a hard object?

Investigation 19

How do earthworms react to different types of surfaces?

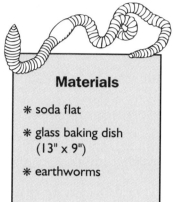

Materials

* soda flat
* glass baking dish (13" x 9")
* earthworms

Place several earthworms at the ends of both a soda flat and a glass baking dish. Observe them for five minutes (see Figure 21).

Observations

On which surface do the earthworms move slowest? How many earthworms reach the other end of the soda flat? Of the glass baking dish?

Discussion

In conducting an experiment, it is important that there is a fair test. This experiment allowed you to compare how an earthworm moves on a smooth surface (glass) versus a rough surface (cardboard). To get meaningful results from an experiment, only one condition or variable should be changed at a time. In this case, the one condition was the surface texture of the container.

The slick glass sometimes results in the earthworm's remaining in a smaller area. Sometimes the earthworm will climb up the side of the cardboard box to avoid the rough surface. Sometimes the mucous layer is rubbed off on the rough surface and makes it more difficult for the earthworm to survive.

Figure 21. A glass baking dish and soda flat provide different surfaces on which an earthworm can move.

Further Investigation

What happens when the end of the box and baking dish are elevated, making an incline for the earthworm to travel?

Investigation 20

How do earthworms react to acid rain?

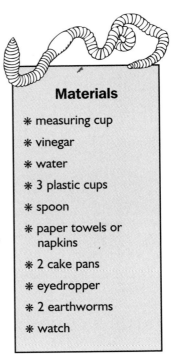

Materials

* measuring cup
* vinegar
* water
* 3 plastic cups
* spoon
* paper towels or napkins
* 2 cake pans
* eyedropper
* 2 earthworms
* watch

Mix about 60 ml (1/4 cup) of vinegar and 250 ml (1 cup) of water in a plastic cup. Stir with a spoon. Since vinegar is a weak acid, this mixture will be considered acid rain. Put about 60 ml (1/4 cup) of water in a second plastic cup and set it off to the side.

Fold 2 paper towels or napkins and place them in the bottom of 2 cake pans. Place three drops of the "acid rain" on one edge of the paper towel in one pan. Rinse the eyedropper thoroughly with plain water. Then place three drops of plain water on one edge of the paper towel in the second pan. Lay one earthworm half on and half off the moist edges of each paper towel, with their heads on the paper towel (see Figure 22). Record how the earthworms react to the acid rain and the plain water. After one minute, pick up the earthworms and dump the one from the acid rain in the plastic cup of plain water to remove the acid rain. Do not rinse the earthworm too long or it will drown. Remove the earthworm and release it in a safe place. Do not put it back into the habitat. Use another earthworm and repeat the experiment, placing the tail halves of the earthworms on the paper towels. Repeat the cleaning and releasing process.

Figure 22. You can prepare weak vinegar water for testing earthworms' reactions to acid rain.

Observations

How did the earthworms react to acid rain compared with plain water? Did they react differently, depending on whether the head or the tail was in the acid rain?

Discussion

Acid rain is a condition that scientists are concerned about. Acidic chemicals from car exhausts and industry smokestacks are sent into the air and return to the earth as acid rain and snow. Acid rain damages buildings and statues; pollutes lakes, streams, and oceans; poisons trees and other plants; and irritates various animals.

Acid rain is a danger to earthworms. It causes the mucous layer to be washed away unless the acid rain is removed with water. Earthworms do not feel pain, but they are able to tell when the environmental conditions are not the best. Their only way to get away from the acid rain is to wiggle away from it. Since earthworms are very slow moving, a heavy acid rain storm can be very harmful to them.

Further Investigations

Repeat the experiment with a weaker acid rain, such as one made from about 60 ml (1/4 cup) vinegar and 500 ml (2 cups) water.

You can also create a solution similar to polluted water by adding two drops of liquid dish detergent to 250 ml (1 cup) of tap water. Repeat the experiment with the "polluted" water. What do you observe? Do not forget to rinse the earthworm with clean water before releasing it.

Investigation 21

How do earthworms react to different odors?

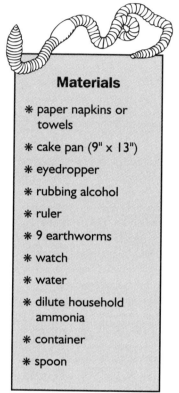

Materials

* paper napkins or towels
* cake pan (9" x 13")
* eyedropper
* rubbing alcohol
* ruler
* 9 earthworms
* watch
* water
* dilute household ammonia
* container
* spoon

Lay a folded napkin or paper towel at one end of a cake pan. Using an eyedropper, add three drops of rubbing alcohol to the edge of the napkin nearest the center of the pan, as shown in Figure 23. Lay the edge of a ruler on the bottom of the pan against the edge of the napkin. Place three earthworms 5 cm (2 in) away from the edge of the napkin. Record where the earthworms are after 1, 3, 5, and 10 minutes.

Repeat the procedure, using water rather than rubbing alcohol. Use different earthworms and a clean pan for this trial.

Next, mix about 60 ml (1/4 cup) of dilute household ammonia in 250 ml (1 cup) of water in a container. Stir with a spoon so that the ammonia and water are well mixed.

Repeat the procedure, using this ammonia mixture rather than rubbing alcohol. Again use different earthworms and a clean pan for this trial.

When finished with the earthworms, rinse them and return them to nature rather than to the habitat. This will prevent contamination of the remaining earthworms if the test earthworms are not completely clean.

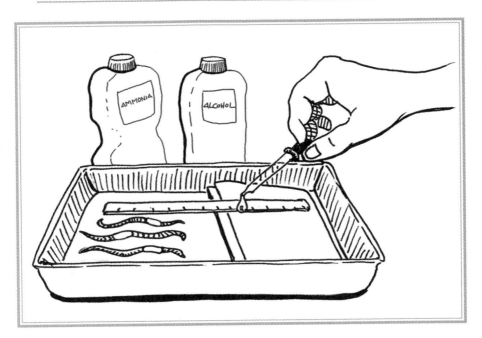

Figure 23. Place a drop of rubbing alcohol at the edge of a folded napkin. What do the earthworms do?

Observations

Where were the earthworms at 1, 3, 5, and 10 minutes when placed near the rubbing alcohol? Ammonia?

Which liquid(s) attracted the earthworms? Which liquid(s) did not attract the earthworms?

Discussion

Earthworms are very sensitive to various odors, even though they do not have noses. They use their skin to detect odors. Earthworms are attracted to the odor of ammonia. Ammonia is naturally released when things decay. Some people put earthworms in their compost piles, since compost is a rich supply of food for earthworms, and the worms help the waste decompose.

Several substances are harmful to earthworms, such as vinegar and rubbing alcohol, because they remove the mucous layer around the body of the earthworm. This layer of mucus allows air and water to enter while keeping out dust and harmful materials. Air and water from the soil enters through very small openings of the skin and goes directly into the earthworm's blood. The water also helps to keep the slimy mucous covering together.

Further Investigation

Repeat the experiment with sweet pickle and dill (sour) pickle juice.

Investigation 22

How do earthworms react to sound vibrations?

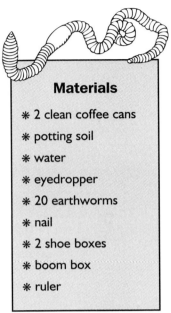

Materials

* 2 clean coffee cans
* potting soil
* water
* eyedropper
* 20 earthworms
* nail
* 2 shoe boxes
* boom box
* ruler

Fill two clean coffee cans up to about 2.5 cm (1 in) from the top with potting soil. Gently press down on the soil with your hand. Add ten drops of water to each can. Lay ten earthworms on the soil of each can (see Figure 24). Using a nail, punch five holes in the bottom of each of two shoe boxes to let air inside. Cover each can with a shoe box, as shown in Figure 25a.

At least six hours later, check to make sure the earthworms have burrowed into the soil. If any earthworms are on top of the soil, remove them. How many earthworms have burrowed?

In another room, check to make sure the boom box works. Turn it off. Set one can with earthworms on the boom box and place the other 15 cm (6 in) away from the boom box, as shown in Figure 25b. Turn on the boom box at a moderate level of volume and record what happens to the earthworms in each can after 1, 3, 5, and 10 minutes. Turn off the boom box and cover the cans with shoe boxes.

Observations

Which can had the most earthworms come out of their burrows? How many earthworms came out of the soil in each can after 1 minute? 3 minutes? 5 minutes? 10 minutes?

Figure 24. Add ten drops of water and ten earthworms to each can of potting soil.

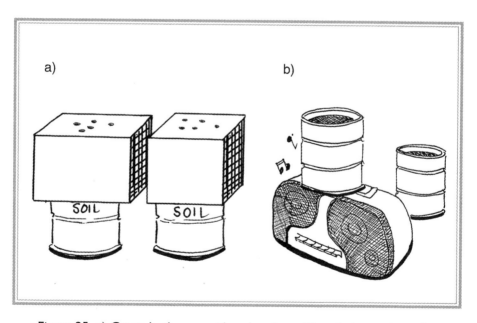

Figure 25. a) Cover both cans with a shoe box. After six hours, have the worms burrowed? b) What happens when the earthworms are exposed to sound vibrations?

Discussion

Sound is the result of vibrations. In this experiment, your boom box was the source of vibrations. Earthworms are very sensitive to vibrations that come through the soil. Even though they do not have ears, their skin can sense the vibrations. It is thought that earthworms come out of the soil when they sense the vibrations to avoid their burrowing enemies, such as moles.

Some people make drumming sounds on the top of the ground to catch earthworms. They have found that frequent drumming in the same place drives the earthworms to the surface for easy collecting. Try it. Does it work for you? What other times do you notice earthworms coming out of their burrows?

Further Investigations

Do burrowed earthworms react differently to classical music than to rock and roll?

Repeat the experiment when a talk show is being played.

Investigation 23

How do earthworms react to red light?

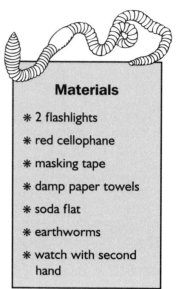

Materials

* 2 flashlights
* red cellophane
* masking tape
* damp paper towels
* soda flat
* earthworms
* watch with second hand

Cover the end of a flashlight with red cellophane. Use masking tape to hold the cellophane in place. Shine the flashlight on a wall to check to see that it works. Place a damp paper towel in a soda flat. Put an earthworm in the center of the box. Darken the room and wait three minutes.

As shown in Figure 26b, shine the flashlight covered with the red cellophane on the earthworm's head for ten seconds. Do the same at the middle and then the tail. Record how the earthworm reacts. Turn off the flashlight for three minutes. Now shine the uncovered flashlight on the earthworm's head, middle, and tail for ten seconds each and record how the earthworm reacts.

Observations

How did the earthworm react when the red-cellophane-covered light was shone on it? When the normal light was shone on it?

Discussion

White light is composed of all the colors in the spectrum: red, orange, yellow, green, blue, indigo, and violet. A rainbow

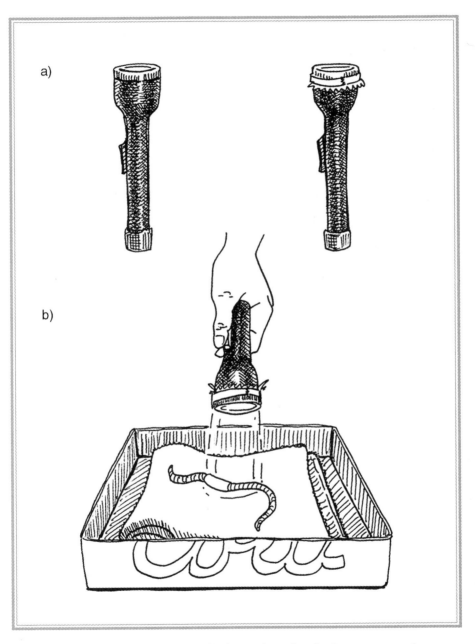

Figure 26. a) Cover one flashlight with red cellophane to test how earthworms react to different colored lights. b) Shine each flashlight onto the earthworm.

occurs when raindrops cause white light to be separated into these seven individual colors. Prisms do the same thing. The red cellophane, though, blocks all colors of the light spectrum from shining through except red. The cellophane can be considered a blocker of the other colors.

Earthworms do not have eyes, but their bodies are sensitive to light. When white light is shone on an earthworm, it will turn away. The light-sensitive region around the head does not react in the same way to the red light.

Further Investigation

Repeat the experiment with yellow, green, and blue cellophane covering the flashlight.

Investigation 24

How does excess water affect earthworms?

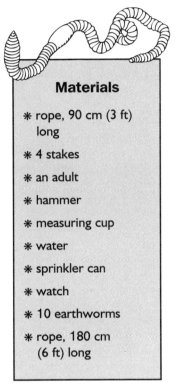

Materials

* rope, 90 cm (3 ft) long
* 4 stakes
* an adult
* hammer
* measuring cup
* water
* sprinkler can
* watch
* 10 earthworms
* rope, 180 cm (6 ft) long

Using a 90-cm (3-ft) length of rope, outline a circle in a bare soil area. Place four stakes along the inside edge of the circle, as shown in Figure 27. Tap the four stakes into the ground with a hammer. The stakes will hold the rope in place. If it has not rained in the past day, use a sprinkler can to add 125 ml (half a cup) of water inside the rope circle. After one hour, release ten earthworms inside the circle.

One day later, count the number of earthworms that are on top of the ground inside the circle. Sprinkle 500 ml (2 cups) of water over the area inside the circle and count how many earthworms crawl onto the surface within 30 minutes.

Using a longer length of rope (180 cm, or 6 ft), make a circle around the smaller circle. If it has not rained, put another 1,000 ml (4 cups) of water in the sprinkler can and sprinkle around inside the larger circle. Count how many earthworms crawl to the surface within 30 minutes.

Observations

How many earthworms are on the surface one day after being released? Are they all within the circles?

Figure 27. How do buried earthworms react to water?

How many earthworms come to the surface after watering inside the smaller circle? Inside the larger circle?

Discussion

As earthworms burrow into the soil, rain will collect in these burrows. Earthworms do not like a lot of water, so they crawl to the surface. The mucous layer on the earthworm helps it survive. Air enters and leaves the earthworm's body through this slimy outer skin. The rain collected in the burrows prevents air movements, so the earthworms crawl to the surface to breathe. This is why you see a lot of earthworms on the ground after it rains. After a rain, you may find dead earthworms on the sidewalk. These earthworms were probably thin and weak due to illnesses. The additional stress caused by the rain was more than their bodies could take.

Sometimes earthworms will burrow on a diagonal rather than straight down, so you may find more earthworms outside the circle than inside the circle. Sometimes you will find more than the ten earthworms you released. Your watering may cause earthworms that had already been established in the area to come to the surface.

Further Investigations

Repeat the experiment on a grassy area.

Repeat the experiment but water only half the circle.

Investigation 25

What other living things are found in the soil?

Materials

* ✳ scissors
* ✳ rubber tubing
* ✳ funnel
* ✳ hot water
* ✳ screw clamp (available at hardware stores)
* ✳ water
* ✳ cheesecloth
* ✳ trowel
* ✳ damp soil
* ✳ cake pan
* ✳ clear glass bowl
* ✳ empty milk jug
* ✳ magnifying glass

Using scissors, cut a 15-cm (6-in) length of rubber tubing. Aquarium tubing works well. Slip one end of the tube over the spout of a funnel. If it is difficult to slip the hose over the spout, place the hose in hot water for 30 seconds and try again. Put a screw clamp on the other end of the hose and tighten it. Pour water into the funnel. If the hose leaks, tighten the clamp until the leak stops. Dump the water. Place a single layer of cheesecloth on the inside of the funnel, as shown in Figure 28a.

Using a trowel, dig a handful of damp soil. Lay out the sample in a cake pan and count how many earthworms and other wiggly animals are in the sample.

Remove the grass from your soil sample and replace the earthworms and other wigglers in the hole that you dug, then put the grass back on top.

Transfer the soil into the funnel. Hold the funnel and hose over a clear glass bowl. Slowly pour water over the soil until the water fills the tube and barely covers the soil. Fold the

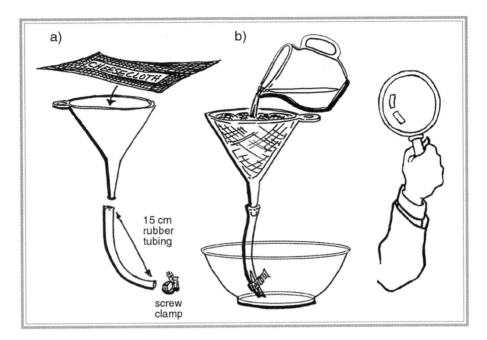

Figure 28. a) With cheesecloth, a funnel, and rubber tubing, make a setup to collect and view soil critters. b) What do you see in the clear glass bowl?

edges of the cheesecloth over the soil and stand the funnel and hose in a milk jug. Put everything in a place where it will not be moved for two days.

Remove the funnel and hose and unscrew the clamp to have the water run into a clear glass bowl, as shown in Figure 28b. Use a magnifying glass to look for small animals in the water. Note their size, shape, color, and other characteristics. Put the soil and water with the animals back in the location that you got them.

Observations

What living things did you notice before putting the soil in the funnel? How did the animals that washed through the hose compare with those you took out of the soil?

Discussion

Frequently when you dig a shovel of soil, several animals will appear. A slightly damp soil sample will often have earthworms and various insects. These insects can either be adults (e.g., ants), larvae or caterpillar (e.g., beetle larvae), or pupae or cocoons (e.g., some moths burrow into the ground to pupate). The longest animal will typically be an earthworm.

The small animals you find in the hose water are nematodes, sometimes called roundworms. These are very active worms that eat soil bacteria and help with decomposition. Some nematodes are very slow wigglers, and they are considered to be plant parasites because they destroy plant roots.

Further Investigations

Prepare a microscope slide of a nematode. Using a microscope, count how many nematodes are in one drop of hose water.

Repeat the experiment, using topsoil and subsoil dug from the same hole.

List of Suppliers

The following companies sell mineral samples, streak plates, and other science supplies. To order materials for your experiments, write or telephone a company to find out about prices. Then send your order to the company with a check or money order to cover the cost. You can also ask your teacher to order materials for you on school stationery.

Carolina Biological Supply
2700 York Road
Burlington, NC 27215
(800) 334-5551
www.carolina.com

Edmund Scientific Company
101 East Gloucester Pike
Barrington, NJ 08007-1380
(609) 573-6250
www.edsu.edu

ETA Science
620 Lakeview Parkway
Vernon Hills, IL 60061
(800) 445-5985
www.etauniverse.com

Fisher Scientific
4901 W. Le Moyne Street
Chicago, IL 60651
(800) 621-4769
www.fishersci.com

Frey Scientific Company

100 Paragon Parkway
Mansfield, OH 44905
(800) 225-3739
www.freyscientific.com

Sargent-Welch/VWR Scientific

P.O. Box 5229
Buffalo Grove, IL 60089–5229
(800) 727-4368
www.SargentWelch.com

Science Kit and Boreal Laboratories

777 East Park Drive
Tonawanda, NY 14150-6782
(800) 828-7777
www.sciencekit.com

Ward's Natural Science Establishment, Inc.

P.O. Box 92912
Rochester, NY 14692–9012
(800) 962-2660
www.wardsci.com

Further Reading

Books

Appelhof, Mary, Mary Frances Fenton, and Barbara Loss Harris. *Worms Eat Our Garbage*. Kalamazoo, Michigan: Flower Press, 1993.

Elsohn Ross, Michael. *Wormology*. Minneapolis: Carolrhoda Books, Inc., 1996.

Hoffman, Jane. *Backyard Scientist Exploring Earthworms with Me: Simple and Fun Experiments to Do with Earthworms*. Irvine, Calif.: Backyard Scientist, Inc., 1994.

Pascoe, Elaine. *Earthworms*. Woodbridge, Conn.: Blackbirch Press, Inc., 1997.

Internet Addresses

"Earthworm FAQ (Reprinted from Green Hut)." *The Compost Resource Page*. n.d. <http://www.oldgrowth.org/compost/wormfaq.html> (July 8, 1999).

Eduzone. "Earthworms, Soil Processes and Plant Growth." *Science Fair Ideas*. n.d. <http://www.eduzone.com/tips/science/gaearth.htm> (July 8, 1999).

NJO. *Worm World*. n.d. <http://www.nj.com/yucky/worm/> (July 8, 1999).

Index